DRINK FROM THE RIVER OF DELIGHT STUDY GUIDE

WELCOME TO GOD'S HEALING SPACE IN HIS WORD

JANET S. ABADIR MD

ISAIAH 61 PUBLISHING

Copyright © 2024 by Janet S. Abadir

All rights reserved.

No portion of this book may be reproduced in any form without written permission from the publisher or author, except as permitted by U.S. copyright law.

The Holy Bible, English Standard Version® (ESV®)
© 2001 by Crossway, a publishing ministry of Good News Publishers.
All rights reserved. The ESV text may not be quoted in any publication made available to the public by a Creative Commons license. The ESV may not be translated in whole or in part into any other language.
ESV Text Edition: 2016

The Holy Bible, English Standard Version (ESV) is adapted from the Revised Standard Version of the Bible, copyright Division of Christian Education of the National Council of the Churches of Christ in the U.S.A. All rights reserved.

Crossway is a not-for-profit organization (a publishing ministry of Good News Publishers) that exists solely for the purpose of publishing the good news of the gospel and the truth of God's Word, the Bible. A portion of the purchase price of every Bible is donated to help support Bible distribution ministry around the world.

Contents

Introduction		1
1.	Chapter 1: You are Thirstier Than You Know: Only One Place to Go	3
2.	Chapter 2: Find Delight in the Bible: Jesus is the Word Made Flesh	13
3.	Chapter 3: The Dry Riverbed of Perfectionism	21
4.	Chapter 4: How to Drink from the River: No Earning, but Effort is Needed	31
5.	Chapter 5: How Drinking from the River Moves Us from Offense to Honor	43
6.	Chapter 6: Delight in Winning: The Aroma of Christ in Suffering	51
7.	Chapter 7: Motivation to Drink Deeply from the River: Rewards are Real	59
8.	Chapter 8: Delight in the Fear of the Lord: A Lifetime of Humility, Joy, and Contentment	67
9.	Chapter 9: Abundant Life in the Body of Christ	77

10.	Chapter 10: Fight Sin with the Gospel: Envy, Discontentment, and Hatred are Toxic to Drink	89
11.	Chapter 11: Treasure Your Treasure: Delight in Jesus Every Day	97
12.	Chapter 12: Glory and Rest in Jesus: This is Where We Belong	105
	Chapter 13: Epilogue	115
	About the author	117
	Drink from the River of Delight	119

Introduction

Welcome to the study guide! Even better, I hope you feel welcomed into God's healing space in His word! Each chapter in the book starts with a Bible passage and ends with a hymn. Make sure you read each Bible passage before you start the questions. You can use these questions as a journal prompt or in a small group discussion. Start out by praying for God to speak to you through His Word, and for your ears to be listening for His voice. Pray for a humble, repentant heart of faith and for eyes to see the truth of the gospel of Jesus Christ. Worship Him for each new truth that you learn. His Word is living and active and will bring about change in your life, because it is the power of God. Let's start our journey with great anticipation and joy, because God is faithful and will keep every promise.

Chapter 1: You are Thirstier than You Know: Only One Place to Go

Read Matthew 12:22-32, and Psalm 95:7-8.

Matthew 12:22-32 "Then a demon-oppressed man who was blind and mute was brought to [Jesus], and he healed him, so that the man spoke and saw. And all the people were amazed, and said, 'Can this man be the Son of David?' But when the Pharisees heard it, they said, 'It is only by Beelzebul, the prince of demons, that this man casts out demons.' Knowing their thoughts, he said to them, 'Every kingdom divided against itself is laid waste, and no city or house divided against itself will stand. And if Satan casts out Satan, he is divided against himself. How then will his kingdom stand? And if I cast out demons by Beelzebul, by whom do your sons cast them out? Therefore they will be your judges. But if it is by the Spirit of God that I cast out demons, then the kingdom of God has come upon you. Or how can someone enter a strong man's house and plunder his goods, unless he first binds the strong man? Then indeed he may plunder his house. Whoever is not with me is against me, and whoever does not gather with me scatters. Therefore I tell you, every sin and blasphemy will be forgiven people, but the blasphemy against the Spirit will not be forgiven. And whoever speaks a word against the Son of Man will be forgiven, but whoever speaks against the Holy Spirit will not be forgiven, either in this age or in the age to come.'"

Psalm 95:7-8 "Today, if you hear his voice, do not harden your hearts."

1. Do you feel alive today? When do you feel most alive? Have you ever felt so numb that you thought your existence was just taking up space? So often we use numbness as a defense mechanism to help ourselves get through a traumatic situation. Ask God to reveal any areas where you have numbed yourself to your feelings. Let Him bring back the sensation right there where it hurts, and see Him change your pain into joyful expectation of redemption. Allow Him to forgive you where you have sinned, and receive that forgiveness. Then ask Him to help you forgive others who may have hurt you as well. Think of Jesus on the cross, refusing to take a numbing sedative, so He could experience the full wrath of God for your sins (Matthew 27:34). Think of His thirst on the cross, and thank Him for being the living water through His death and resurrection for you.

2. Are you in control of your emotions? Sometimes you have to preach to your heart because emotions may feel like the truth, but they can be misleading. Overwhelming emotions will pass, but the Word of God will stand forever. When emotions are strong, take a deep breath and relocate yourself into God's safe, healing space of freedom. You are not a slave to sin, and God is greater than your emotions. Look at God's emotions in Psalm 95, and realize that through Jesus, you bring joy to God's heart as you worship Him and respond with obedience. Pray for people who have hard hearts towards God so that they can hear His voice today and respond in faith.

3. What is oppressing you today? Is it guilt or shame from your past? Is it regret over what you never accomplished? Is it your own sins of unforgiveness and unbelief? You could also be oppressed by a demonic influence. Pray aloud in the name of Jesus for freedom from these influences, and look at the cross as the answer to all these concerns. Remember your union with Christ: His past is your past, His future is your future, and in the present you are empowered by Christ and clothed with Christ.

4. Who brings you to Jesus when you are powerless to go to Him yourself? The Holy Spirit's role in our lives is to constantly bring us to Jesus. There are humans who can help too! Think of who that is for you, and say a prayer thanking God for them. Reach out to them and let them know you appreciate them always leading you back to Jesus.

5. Do you see your need for Jesus today? We are more thirsty than we know! When we don't feel thirsty for Jesus, it's usually because we have allowed sin into our hearts. Pray for God to reveal any hardness of heart or unbelief in your life so you can feel your need for Jesus. Enjoy the promise of God to supply all your needs from His infinite riches in Christ (Philippians 4:19).

6. Sin makes us blind. The more we sin, the more blind we become. Ask God to heal your spiritual sight so that you can see the sin in your life and repent. Sin is more than outward actions—sin starts in your heart. It is any rebellion against God, and any unbelief regarding His Word. It is wanting your will more than you want God's will. Start each day praying, "I delight to do Your will, O God, please put your law of love into my heart"(see Psalm 40). Remember that the way to your heart is through your ears, so keep listening to the word of God all day long.

7. Worship God for freeing you from demonic oppression. Satan is a defeated enemy. Jesus has bound Satan and is plundering his possessions by saving people through the gospel. Declare your allegiance to Jesus Christ. How can you share this message with someone who needs it? Thank Jesus for being the kindest and most loving King of Kings, and Lord of Lords, who endured Satan's oppression and defeated him for all eternity.

Come Ye Sinners, Poor and Needy by Joseph Hart

Come ye sinners, poor and needy, weak and wounded, sick and sore;
Jesus ready stands to save you, full of pity, love and pow'r.

Come ye thirsty, come and welcome, God's free bounty glorify;
true belief and true repentance, every grace that brings you nigh.

Let not conscience make you linger, nor of fitness fondly dream;
all the fitness He requireth is to feel your need of Him.

Come ye weary, heavy laden, lost and ruined by the fall;
if you tarry till you're better, you will never come at all.

Lo! th'incarnate God, ascended, pleads the merit of His blood;
venture on Him, venture wholly; let no other trust intrude.

Chapter 2: Find Delight in the Bible: Jesus is the Word Made Flesh

Read Psalm 107:17-22, Psalm 119:103, and John 1:14.

Psalm 107:17-22 "Some were fools through their sinful ways, and because of their iniquities suffered affliction; they loathed any kind of food, and they drew near to the gates of death. Then they cried to the LORD in their trouble, and he delivered them from their distress. He sent out his word and healed them and delivered them from their destruction. Let them thank the LORD for his steadfast love, for his wondrous works to the children of man!"

Psalm 119:103 "How sweet are your words to my taste, sweeter than honey to my mouth!"

John 1:14 "And the Word became flesh and dwelt among us, and we have seen his glory, glory as of the only Son from the Father, full of grace and truth."

1. Do you believe that the Bible is the Word of God? Does the exclusivity of Jesus' claims bother you (He is the **only** way, truth, and life- John 14:6)? Has He done enough to prove that He is who He said He was? What is holding you back from surrendering your heart and life to Jesus? The resurrection of Jesus Christ is the answer to all your doubts and fears—Jesus has resurrected from the dead, now and for eternity He has a glorified human body, and He will return to earth one day. Read Acts 17:22-31, and be assured that the resurrected Jesus will judge all men and women someday. No human being could make this story up. Pray a prayer of surrender to God's Word and God's authority.

2. Has God ever spoken to you and created something in your life? If you have faith in Jesus, that faith was given to you by God. Think of when Jesus calmed the storm in Mark 4:39. All He had to do was say, "Peace! Be still!" and the wind ceased, and there was a great calm. Ask Jesus to speak peace to your heart today. "And [Jesus] came and preached peace to you who were far off and peace to those who were near" (Ephesians 2:17). You can grow in your faith by hearing His voice: "So faith comes from hearing, and hearing through the word of Christ" (Romans 10:17).

3. Where are you holding back from complete surrender to God? You can find out by analyzing the times you were overwhelmed with fear, anger, or anxiety. What was the thing in that situation that was threatened? That thing may be something you are holding on to more than God. It could be your reputation, your productivity, your family, or your income. You might be finding your identity and significance in those things. Repent and see that God is what you are really longing for, and when you surrender to Him, you can live in wisdom towards all those other things.

4. Do you realize that you have been called by God? Do you think of yourself as holy to God (set apart for a specific purpose, bringing glory to God through your love, worship, and obedience)? How can you keep this in the forefront of your thoughts today? It's your calling from God that makes you great, and you already have that. You serve a great God, so don't worry about doing great things for Him because everything you do for Him is great (Hebrews 3:6).

5. Have you ever fallen into the pattern of trying to fix your own sins? Do you run to God or away from God when you sin? Read Psalm 32 and see the forgiveness God offers you through Jesus. Rejoice in your forgiveness and the blessedness of never having to hide from God again.

6. Do you read your Bible every day? Why or why not? Do you think of the Bible as a vitamin supplement that is good for you to take or do you see it as an essential life-saving medication? Start with just a few verses every day and write down what God says to you in a journal. Pray for God to do the work of making these verses true in your life. The Bible is all about Jesus, and He is the power you need to change. Ask Him to give you a hunger for His Word. If you are using something else to feed your soul, repent and rejoice that God is so satisfying.

Speak, O Lord by Keith Getty and Stuart Townend

Speak, O Lord, as we come to You to receive the food of Your Holy Word.
Take Your truth, plant it deep in us
shape and fashion us in Your likeness
that the light of Christ might be seen today
in our acts of love and our deeds of faith.
Speak, O Lord, and fulfill in us all your purposes for your glory.

Teach us Lord, full obedience, Holy reverence, true humility.
Test our thoughts and our attitudes
in the radiance of Your purity.
Cause our faith to rise, cause our eyes to see
Your majestic love and authority.
Words of pow'r that can never fail,
let their truth prevail over unbelief.

Speak O Lord, and renew our minds
help us grasp the heights of Your plans for us.
Truths unchanged from the dawn of time
that will echo down through eternity.
And by grace we'll stand on Your promises,
and by faith we'll walk as You walk with us.
Speak, O Lord, till Your church is built
and the earth is filled with Your glory.

Chapter 3: The Dry Riverbed of Perfectionism

Read Psalm 25.

Psalm 25 "To you, O LORD, I lift up my soul. O my God, in you I trust; let me not be put to shame; let not my enemies exult over me. Indeed, none who wait for you shall be put to shame; they shall be ashamed who are wantonly treacherous. Make me to know your ways, O LORD; teach me your paths. Lead me in your truth and teach me, for you are the God of my salvation; for you I wait all the day long. Remember your mercy, O LORD, and your steadfast love, for they have been from of old. Remember not the sins of my youth or my transgressions; according to your steadfast love remember me, for the sake of your goodness O LORD! Good and upright is the LORD; therefore he instructs sinners in the way. He leads the humble in what is right, and teaches the humble his way. All the paths of the LORD are steadfast love and faithfulness, for those who keep his covenant and his testimonies. For your name's sake, O LORD, pardon my guilt, for it is great. Who is the man who fears the LORD? Him will he instruct in the way that he should choose. His soul shall abide in well-being, and his offspring shall inherit the land. The friendship of the LORD is for those who fear him, and he makes known to them his covenant. My eyes are ever toward the LORD, for he will pluck my feet out of the net. Turn to me and be gracious to me, for I am lonely and afflicted. The troubles of my heart are enlarged; bring me out of my distresses. Consider my affliction and my trouble, and forgive all my sins. Consider how many are my foes, and with what violent hatred they hate me. Oh guard my soul, and deliver me! Let me not be put to shame, for I take refuge in you. May integrity and uprightness preserve me, for I wait for you. Redeem Israel, O God, out of all his troubles."

1. Shame is crushing. Shame causes you to look away from others. You may feel like trash. You think of all the times people treated you as trash and you believe that the people were correct. The Bible has good news for those struggling with shame—you are indeed broken by sin, but you are **not** trash. Jesus took your shame and sin on the cross. He now looks into your eyes, gazes at your face, and beams His love, acceptance, and honor at you. Read 2 Corinthians 3:16-18, and see the glory of God in the loving face of Jesus Christ. The more you gaze at Jesus and receive His love and forgiveness, the more freedom from shame you will experience, and the more you will have courage to reach out to others with His love and forgiveness.

2. How is Jesus your friend? Read John 15. All human friends have limits on how far they will let you into their hearts. But now, picture Jesus' heart being all the way open to you. He will not hold back His heart from you. Ask Him to show you more of His heart for you and others. Ask Him to make you a faithful friend to others.

3. Perfectionists hate to fail. Perfectionists are always disappointed with themselves and others. Perfectionists are always worried about measuring up. Do you think this is a healthy way to live? Does God expect you to be perfect? What is the path of life that God offers us? (Hint- righteousness in Christ, not in your performance) Remember that God redeems our failures and turns them into good in the end (Romans 8:28).

4. Where do you find rest? Perfectionists feel guilty when they need to rest. They are upset when they reach their limits. Humility is coming to our limits and then worshipping our God of no limits. Praise God for the true rest He offers us in Christ: rest from performance-based worth, rest from earning, rest from proving ourselves, and rest from worry about the outcome of our lives. He is glorified when we are satisfied in Him, enjoying His presence and good gifts to us (Psalm 16).

5. Have you struggled with procrastination? Starting a new project is more intimidating if you expect perfection from yourself. Ask God for the courage and humility to obey. We can delight to do God's will now because the Holy Spirit lives inside us. Listen to what God is telling you to do right now. Do that thing, then do the next thing He leads you to. He usually doesn't tell you the big picture, but gives you one step at a time. If you look back on your life, you will see His guidance so clearly. Praise Him for leading you every day! (Proverbs 3)

6. What does waiting on God mean? Is it a passive, fatalistic type of waiting, or an active waiting in faith? Is God asking you to wait about something in your life? How can you lift up your soul to God in this moment, and not lift up your soul to anything else? God will keep all His promises to you, and you will receive every good thing from Him, either in this life or in the next! Read Psalm 40 and Hebrews 12 for more help with waiting on God.

All Sufficient Merit by Bethany Barnard, Bryan Fowler, Shane Barnard
All sufficient merit shining like the sun,
a fortune I inherit by no work I have done.
My righteousness I forfeit at my Savior's cross,
where all sufficient merit did what I could not.

In love He condescended eternal now in time,
a life without a blemish the Maker made to die.
The law could never save us, our lawlessness had won,
until the pure and spotless Lamb had finally come.

It is done, it is finished, no more debt I owe.
Paid in full, all-sufficient merit now my own.

I lay down my garments, any empty boast.
Good works now all corrupted by the sinful host,
dressed in my Lord Jesus, a crimson robe made white,
no more fear of judgment: His righteousness is mine.

All sufficient merit, firm in life and death.
The joy of my salvation shall be my final breath.
When I stand accepted before the throne of God,
I'll gaze upon my Jesus and thank Him for the cross.

Chapter 4: How to Drink from the River: No Earning, but Effort is Needed

Read 1 Corinthians 1:26-31 and Psalm 36:7-9.

1 Corinthians 1:26-31 "For consider your calling, brothers: not many of you were wise according to worldly standards, not many were powerful, not many were of noble birth. But God chose what is foolish in the world to shame the wise; God chose what is weak in the world to shame the strong; God chose what is low and despised in the world, even things that are not, to bring to nothing things that are, so that no human being might boast in the presence of God. And because of him you are in Christ Jesus, who became to us wisdom from God, righteousness and sanctification and redemption, so that, as it is written, 'Let the one who boasts, boast in the Lord.'"

Psalm 36:7-9 "How precious is your steadfast love, O God! The children of mankind take refuge in the shadow of your wings. They feast on the abundance of your house, and you give them drink from the river of your delights. For with you is the fountain of life; in your light do we see light."

1. Have you ever had something blow up in your face, or not get the outcome you were expecting? Were you angry? Humble people know that every good thing comes from God (James 1:17), not themselves, so when things don't go as planned they can laugh and rejoice that God's plans are never thwarted. Grumbling comes from dashed expectations and entitlement. If you are suffering, groan to God, and go to Him in faith as His beloved child, instead of grumbling and questioning His love and presence with you.

2. How have you been trying to earn your salvation? Do you keep score of your good deeds so they can outweigh your bad deeds? Do you compare your performance with other Christians? Do you like to feel superior to other people? Are you plagued with feelings of inferiority? All of these are signs that you are not fully trusting in Jesus to save you. Release your hope of "fixing" yourself, receive Jesus' all-powerful blood which cleanses you, and rejoice in your new freedom from comparison, score-keeping, and self-righteousness. Worship God for His steadfast love.

3. What do you know about the fear of the Lord? Have you ever thought of the fear of the Lord replacing all your other fears (Isaiah 8:11-13)? What does that mean to you? Have you ever let the fear of man control your decision-making? How did that turn out? Pray that God reveals any fear of man you may be living under, so that He can free you from it and give you the proper, delightful, fear of the Lord instead (Nehemiah 1:11).

4. How would you define humility? Think of Jesus' humility in taking the lowest position so that we can enjoy the highest position of welcome into God's family. Humility means thinking of others' needs ahead of your own. It means enjoying other people's victories as much as you would have had it been you. Encounters with humble people leave others feeling appreciated, listened to, and respected, even if the two disagree. Make an effort to appreciate humility in others. Repent of your pride and ask God for humility. See your own limits as an opportunity to worship our God of no limits.

5. Meekness isn't weakness. Jesus was meek, but He is all-powerful at the same time. Meekness is the "secret sauce" of wisdom and maturity in Christ. Do you want meekness? Do you admire it in others? Read Psalm 37:9,11, James 1:21, James 3:13, and 1 Peter 2:22. See how meekness involves waiting on the Lord, receiving His Word as our exclusive source of wisdom and truth to obey, and allowing God to be our vindication instead of ourselves. Worship God that the meek will inherit the earth. Praise Jesus for showing us the beauty of meekness.

6. Have you tried to die to your flesh and live in the power of the Spirit? Read Romans 8, Colossians 3, and Galatians 5. What are the works of the flesh? You can also think of the flesh as self-justifying behavior (maybe even going to church to make you look good!), in addition to the obvious sinful, worldly behavior. What does living in the Spirit look like? How can you put off the flesh and put on Christ each day? This is impossible to do just by will-power: you need to ask for Holy Spirit power! Compliment someone on the fruit of the Spirit that you see in their life.

7. What inspires you to worship and praise God? If you don't understand how sinful you are, you won't appreciate the grace of God and the free gift of salvation. If your heart doesn't naturally worship God throughout the day, you aren't very self-aware of your desperate need for God and His delight in helping you. Repent of your lack of worship, and ask God to help you boast in Christ. Make sure that your boasting is in Christ and not in yourself. God is the fountain of life, light, and delight!

8. Next time you are tempted to feel angry, frustrated, or grumpy, try to think of the perfect record you already have in Christ, and the eternal glory that awaits you. God has compassion for you. He is pleased with you in Christ and rejoices over you with singing. Remember and breathe in contentment, peace with God, hope, and joy. Release (what you are holding on to-good or bad), receive (the better things in Jesus), and rejoice. (I use the analogy of getting your hand stuck in the cookie jar. You have to let go of the cookie to get your hand out. Then your hand is free to receive something better, and you can rejoice!)

Our Pleasure and Our Duty by John Newton

Our pleasure and our duty, though opposite before,
since we have seen His beauty are joined to part no more.

To see the law by Christ fulfilled and hear His pardoning voice,
transforms a slave into a child, and duty into choice.

Chapter 5: How Drinking from the River Moves Us from Offense to Honor

R ead 1 Peter 1:22-2:8.

1 Peter 1:22-2:8 "Having purified your souls by your obedience to the truth for a sincere brotherly love, love one another earnestly from a pure heart, since you have been born again, not of perishable seed but of imperishable, through the living and abiding word of God; for 'All flesh is like grass and all its glory like the flower of the grass. The grass withers, and the flower falls, but the word of the Lord remains forever.' And this word is the good news that was preached to you. So put away all malice and all deceit and hypocrisy and envy and all slander. Like newborn infants, long for the pure spiritual milk, that by it you may grow up into salvation- if indeed you have tasted that the Lord is good. As you come to him, a living stone rejected by men but in the sight of God chosen and precious, you yourselves like living stones are being built up as a spiritual house, to be a holy priesthood, to offer spiritual sacrifices acceptable to God through Jesus Christ. For it stands in Scripture: 'Behold, I am laying in Zion a stone, a cornerstone, chosen and precious, and whoever believes in him will not be put to shame.' So the honor is for you who believe, but for those who do not believe, 'The stone that the builders rejected has become the

cornerstone,' and 'A stone of stumbling, and a rock of offense.' They stumble because they disobey the word, as they were destined to do."

1. Do you hate starting over like I do? What circumstances in your life take the wind out of your sails and deflate your hopes and dreams? Are you easily offended? Meditate on the honor you have already in Christ, and your certain hope of glory, seeing Jesus face-to-face. Though you have not seen Him, you love Him and rejoice with joy filled with glory, receiving the outcome of your faith, the salvation of your soul (1 Peter 1:8-9)!

2. Have you ever thought about the Trinity, one God, Three Persons? Why is this an essential doctrine of our faith? The beauty of relationship is the essence of our God. Beautiful relationships are like a dance where we orbit around each other rather than forcing others to orbit around our needs alone. What relationships in your life are in a healthy dance? Do you see unhealthy patterns in some of your relationships? Ask God for wisdom and grace to bring peace, forgiveness, and grace into all your relationships. God has compassion for us, and loves to shower our relationships with compassion and grace, covering over a multitude of our sins (1 Peter 4:8). Some relationships may not be reparable in this life, but as far as it depends on you, live at peace with one another (Romans 12:18).

3. What is the purpose of suffering? One benefit of suffering is that it demonstrates to us that the visible world is passing away, but the word of the Lord stands forever. Worship God for His permanence, His unchanging nature, and His faithfulness. Read Hebrews 1:10-12, quoting Psalm 102. Relocate your security and hope in God, not your circumstances.

4. Do you see any value in the suffering that you have endured? If you are having a hard time with this, think of the value of Jesus' suffering for you. He was rejected and despised and afflicted, and the outcome of His suffering was your salvation and redemption, and ultimate glory to God. You can rejoice that God will get the maximum glory from your life. Remember Jesus' motivation: the joy set before Him (Hebrews 12:2). Let the joy of the Lord be your strength (Nehemiah 8:10), because you belong to the Lord and He is with you in your suffering.

5. How are we like living stones built on Christ? Look at Ephesians 2:11-22, and the analogy Paul makes of the Church being built on the foundation of Christ, and all of us joined together as a holy temple to the Lord, the dwelling place for God by the Spirit. Can you be an isolated stone? How can you form more connections to the Body of Christ? Worship God for living inside you now and for eternity.

How Firm a Foundation by John Rippon

How firm a foundation, ye saints of the Lord, is laid for your faith in His excellent Word!

What more can He say than to you He hath said. To you who for refuge to Jesus have fled?

Fear not, I am with thee, O be not dismayed, for I am thy God and will still give thee aid;

I'll strengthen thee, help thee, and cause thee to stand, upheld by My righteous, omnipotent hand.

When through the deep waters I call thee to go, the rivers of sorrow shall not overflow;

for I will be with thee, thy troubles to bless, and sanctify to thee thy deepest distress.

When through fiery trials thy pathway shall lie, my grace, all sufficient, shall be thy supply;

the flame shall not hurt thee; I only design thy dross to consume, and thy gold to refine.

E'en down to old age all My people shall prove My sovereign, eternal, unchangeable love;

and then, when grey hairs shall their temples adorn, like lambs they shall still in My bosom be borne.

The soul that on Jesus hath leaned for repose, I will not, I will not desert to his foes;

that soul, though all hell should endeavor to shake, I'll never, no never, no never forsake!

Chapter 6: Delight in Winning: The Aroma of Christ in Suffering

Read 2 Corinthians 2:14-17 and Psalm 68:1-3 and 18-20.

2 Corinthians 2: 14-17 "But thanks be to God, who in Christ always leads us in triumphal procession, and through us spreads the fragrance of the knowledge of him everywhere. For we are the aroma of Christ to God among those who are being saved and among those who are perishing, to one a fragrance from death to death, to the other a fragrance from life to life. Who is sufficient for these things? For we are not, like so many, peddlers of God's word, but as men of sincerity, as commissioned by God, in the sight of God we speak in Christ."

Psalm 68: 1-3, 18-20 "God shall arise, his enemies shall be scattered; and those who hate him shall flee before him! As smoke is driven away, so you shall drive them away; as wax melts before fire, so the wicked shall perish before God! But the righteous shall be glad; they shall exult before God; they shall be jubilant with joy! You ascended on high, leading a host of captives in your train and receiving gifts among men, even among the rebellious, that the LORD God may dwell there. Blessed be the LORD, who daily bears us up; God is our salvation.

Our God is a God of salvation, and to GOD, the Lord, belong deliverances from death."

1. When did you feel most honored in your life? What does winning mean to you? How much of your energy and effort is spent on trying to win? How would your life change if you defined winning as pleasing God through faith, obedience, and delight in Him?

2. When have you experienced the most shame and rejection from others? How did you cope with those feelings? Did you make any vows to yourself so that you would never have to endure that again? Do you think that being a Christian is compatible with experiencing shame and rejection? Relocate your identity into Christ who was rejected, but who is now seated on the throne of the universe, and who is your High Priest and Intercessor. Let go of unhealthy vows, because you are ultimately safe in Jesus (Psalm 91).

3. Do you feel like you are in the front of Christ's victory parade (prisoner of war on display) or the back (a soldier in the conquering army)? Looking back on your life, can you see seasons of honor and blessing, mixed with seasons of grief and rejection? It's so liberating to realize that both are part of God's plan for His children. Either way, we focus on Christ, the conquering King and Captain of the army. Don't think of Jesus as being on your team, but see yourself as being on Jesus' team. He is in charge, not you, and you can trust Him to do what's best for you. Encourage someone you know who is going through a difficult season by sharing these truths with them.

4. Have you told someone about God's work in your life today? Sharing your story of God's faithfulness in your suffering will encourage your fellow believers to persevere through trials and difficulties. Think of a 30-second "elevator speech" you can give about God rescuing you and winning the victory in a specific instance, and ask God for opportunities to share that with others today.

5. Do you exaggerate or omit details when you tell stories about yourself? All of us use a little "spin" to make ourselves look better to others. Let's remember the humiliation and agony of Jesus being paraded through Jerusalem carrying His cross for us, so that we can drop our pretense and be genuine and vulnerable with others. Jesus is now highly exalted and given the name that is above every name—likewise we are honored in Him already. This truth will help you be courageous in putting the real YOU out there and forming deep connections with other people for the glory of God.

Jesus, Thy Head, Once Crowned by Thomas Kelly

Jesus, Thy head, once crowned with thorns, is crowned with glory now;
Heav'n's royal diadem adorns the mighty Victor's brow!

Thou glorious light of courts above, joy of the saints below,
to us still manifest Thy love, that we its depths may know.

To us Thy cross with all its shame, with all its grace be giv'n;
tho' earth disowns Thy lowly name, God honors it in heav'n.

Who suffer with Thee, Lord, below, shall reign with Thee above;
then let it be our joy to know this way of peace and love.

To us Thy cross is life and health; 'twas shame and death to Thee;
our present glory, joy and wealth, our everlasting stay.

Chapter 7: Motivation to Drink Deeply from the River: Rewards are Real

Read Colossians 3:1-4.

Colossians 3:1-4 "If then you have been raised with Christ, seek the things that are above, where Christ is, seated at the right hand of God. Set your minds on things that are above, not on things that are on earth. For you have died and your life is hidden with Christ in God. When Christ who is your life appears, then you also will appear with him in glory."

1. What motivates you to serve Jesus? Do you worry about what people are thinking about you? Our default motives can be fear or pride, but the gospel gives us a new motivation. We can please God by faith in Jesus! We can bring delight to God's heart, as we delight in serving him. "As for the saints in the land, they are the excellent ones, in whom is all my delight" (Psalm 16:3).

2. What is glory? One definition is great honor, distinction, renown, praise, and admiration. Have you thought about where you may be receiving glory from other people (John 5:44)? Sometimes you are unaware of the effects of man's glory on you until you stop receiving it and you miss it dearly. Where do you feel the most susceptible to wanting man's glory? How can you turn your attention to God's glory and God's kingdom in that moment? Man's glory is fleeting, and only God's glory lasts. "But you, O LORD, are a shield about me, my glory, and the lifter of my head" (Psalm 3:3). Praise God for the glory that awaits you in Christ!

3. Do you see abundance or scarcity around you? If your physical eyes are telling you something contrary to the reality in the Bible, then ask God for His wisdom to change your perspective. Once I read Psalm 37 over and over again with tears, because I could not "see" how it could be true, even though I knew it was God's Word. God will speak through His Word, and will change your heart and mind. When I am overwhelmed with scarcity, I may need to go to a friend and pray through Scripture together. Fellowship in the Body of Christ is essential to maintain my faith in God and His Word.

4. Do you live for rewards? That is a good thing if you are living for the right rewards! The biblical view of rewards is astonishing. Every time you love and serve someone in the Body of Christ, you are gaining an eternal reward in God's kingdom. Jesus even went so far as to say that rewards are transferable: "The one who receives a prophet because he is a prophet will receive a prophet's reward, and the one who receives a righteous person because he is a righteous person will receive a righteous person's reward" (Matthew 10:41). This is the key to serving others without grumbling. Rewards aren't received at the expense or to the exclusion of others, but we benefit together from all the rewards in the Body of Christ. Ask God for opportunities to serve others especially in the Body of Christ.

5. What does "Union with Christ" mean? Colossians 3:1-4 is all true of Christ—He died, He was raised from the dead, and now He has ascended to the throne of the universe. Now it is all true of us—we have died to sin and the flesh, now we are raised up in resurrection life and power, and we will ascend to be with Him in glory. We can even think of ourselves as seated there with Him right now (Ephesians 2:6-7). Try to think about union with Christ all day long. It's like you are a newlywed and Christ is your Husband. He is patiently waiting for the day that He will see you face-to-face.

Hail, Thou Once Despised Jesus! By John Bakewell

Hail, Thou once despised Jesus!
Hail, Thou still rejected King.
Thou didst suffer to release us, Thou didst free salvation bring.
Thro' Thy death and resurrection, bearer of our sin and shame!
We enjoy divine protection, life and glory through Thy name.

Paschal Lamb, by God appointed, all our sins on Thee were laid.
By our Father's love anointed, Thou hast full atonement made.
All who trust Thee are forgiven thro' the virtue of Thy blood;
Rent in Thee the vail of heaven,
grace shines forth to man from God.

Saviour hail! Amid the glory, where for us Thou dost abide;
we, by faith do now adore Thee, seated at Thy Father's side.
There for us Thou now art pleading,
while Thou dost are place prepare;
for Thy saints still interceding, till in glory we appear.

Worship, honor, praise and blessing,
Thou shalt then from all receive;
loudest praises without ceasing, all that earth or heav'n can give:
in that day Thy saints will meet Thee,
welcome Thee with grateful song;
joyful hearts will ever greet Thee,
source of joy to all the throng!

Chapter 8: Delight in the Fear of the Lord: A Lifetime of Humility, Joy, and Contentment

Read Jeremiah 17:5-14.

Jeremiah 17:5-14 "Thus says the LORD: 'Cursed is the man who trusts in man and makes flesh his strength, whose heart turns away from the LORD. He is like a shrub in the desert, and shall not see any good come. He shall dwell in the parched places of the wilderness, in an uninhabited salt land. Blessed is the man who trusts in the LORD, whose trust is the LORD. He is like a tree planted by water, that sends out its roots by the stream, and does not fear when heat comes, for its leaves remain green, and is not anxious in the year of drought, for it does not cease to bear fruit.' The heart is deceitful above all things, and desperately sick; who can understand it? 'I the LORD search the heart and test the mind, to give every man according to the fruit of his deeds.' Like the partridge that gathers a brood that she did not hatch, so is he who gets riches but not by justice; in the midst of his days they will leave him, and at his end he will be a fool. A glorious throne set on high from the beginning is the place of our sanctuary. O LORD, the hope of Israel, all who forsake you shall be put to shame; those who turn away from you shall be written in the earth, for they have forsaken the LORD, the fountain of living water. Heal me O LORD, and I shall be healed; save me, and I shall be saved, for you are my praise."

1. What is the fear of the Lord? Everyone lives in the fear of something. Fear in this context means giving something the highest authority in your life, and the only two options are God or something God has created. God created mankind, so giving man's wisdom the highest authority in your life over God is truly foolishness. The fear of the Lord also involves the acknowledgment that God's wrath is the most terrifying thing you can ever imagine. When you see Jesus bearing God's wrath for you on the cross, you begin to understand that the fear of the Lord is actually your delight (Isaiah 11:3).

2. Contrast the two kinds of people mentioned in Jeremiah 17. Do you ever tell yourself that you are cursed? Do you use your words to curse? God curses the man who trusts in man and who turns away from the Lord in his heart. We were all under God's curse because of our sin until Jesus took our curse by dying on the cross (Galatians 3:10-14). You can have God's blessing for eternity by turning back to the Lord. Thank God for all His blessings. Use your words to bless and not to curse because you are now blessed and not cursed! Thank you Jesus!

3. What is the difference between trusting in the Lord and trusting in man (including yourself)? The modern "self-help" movement is twisted and deceptive. You cannot find help in yourself, but only in God. Repent of believing the lies of our culture: I am enough, I am worthy (in myself), you do you, I am the captain of my soul, I am in control. The gospel truth is that God is enough and God gives you enough, God is worthy of your worship and praise and He gives you His righteousness and worthiness in Christ, God is the Judge and what you do matters for eternity, God is the Captain of your soul, and God is in control of everything, even your choices. Let's ask God for His help in all these things! He will help you make good and wise choices and He will be your hope of standing on judgment day.

4. Have you ever followed your heart? What happened? Jeremiah 17:9 says that the most defining characteristic of your heart is deceit. Further, it says that your heart is desperately sick. Your heart is twisted by your sin nature which you inherited from Adam. The worst part of this heart sickness is that we are blind to it. We think we have a good heart because we are "good people." The Bible says that "every intention of the thoughts of [man's] heart was only evil continually" (Genesis 6:5). Your heart is good at making idols and worshiping them. Your heart is good at holding on to hatred and resentment. Your heart is good at being selfish and prideful. Ask God to show you the deceitfulness of your own heart so that He can heal you and give you His wisdom and faithfulness instead. Praise God that He gives us a new heart in Christ (Ezekiel 36:26, 2 Corinthians 5:17).

5. How can you find your sanctuary in God's glorious throne (Jeremiah 17:12)? A sanctuary is a safe haven, a place to run when you are in danger. You usually run somewhere when you are in trouble. Run to God's glorious throne. It has been your sanctuary from the beginning. It is holy, positioned above everything in this world. It is where God is ruling over everything. You have the ear of the Lord of the universe. "Let us then with confidence draw near to the throne of grace, that we may receive mercy and find grace to help in time of need"(Hebrews 4:16).

6. Do you see God as your healer (Jeremiah 17:14)? You are going somewhere for your healing all the time. Are you hoping in modern medicine, or exercise, or dieting, or self-help? You can utilize good healing techniques, but they are not your hope. Only God is your hope of healing and salvation, and so He must also be your praise and boasting. Tell a story to others of God's healing in your life.

Nothing Either Great or Small by James Proctor

Nothing either great or small- nothing, sinner, no,
Jesus did it, did it all, long, long ago.

"It is finished," yes indeed, finished, every jot:
sinner this is all you need-tell me is it not?

When He, from His lofty throne, stooped to do and die,
everything was fully done; hearken to His cry.

Weary, working burdened one, wherefore toil you so?
Cease your doing, all was done, long, long ago.

Till to Jesus' work you cling by a simple faith,
"Doing" is a deadly thing, "doing ends in death.

Cast your deadly "doing" down- down at Jesus' feet;
stand in Him, in Him alone, gloriously complete.

Chapter 9: Abundant Life in the Body of Christ

Read Ephesians 4.

Ephesians 4:1-16 "I therefore, a prisoner for the Lord, urge you to walk in a manner worthy of the calling to which you have been called, with all humility and gentleness, with patience, bearing with one another in love, eager to maintain the unity of the Spirit in the bond of peace. There is one body and one Spirit- just as you were called to the one hope that belongs to your call- one Lord, one faith, one baptism, one God and Father of all, who is over all and through all and in all. But grace was given to each one of us according to the measure of Christ's gift. Therefore it says, 'When he ascended on high he led a host of captives, and he gave gifts to men.' (In saying, 'He ascended,' what does it mean but that he had also descended into the lower regions, the earth? He who descended is the one who also ascended far above all the heavens, that he might fill all things.) And he gave the apostles, the prophets, the evangelists, the shepherds and teachers, to equip the saints for the work of ministry, for building up the body of Christ, until we all attain to the unity of the faith and of the knowledge of the Son of God, to mature manhood, to the measure of the stature of the fullness of the Christ, so that we may no longer be children, tossed to and fro by the waves and carried about by every wind of doctrine, by human cunning, by craftiness in deceitful schemes. Rather, speaking the truth in love, we are to grow up in every way into him who is the head, into Christ, from whom the whole body, joined and held together by every joint with which it is equipped, when each part is working properly, makes the body grow so that it builds itself up in love."

1. Do you see the value of the Body of Christ? Do you see Christian relationships as an asset or a liability? If you say you love Jesus, then you are obligated to love every other believer in Jesus because Jesus lives in them just like He lives in you. Indifference is not an option. Pray that God would help you cheer for all your brothers and sisters in Christ.

2. The Apostle Paul describes himself as a prisoner of the Lord. Paul saw his imprisonment as the result of God's sovereignty, not because of Roman arrest. God's sovereignty means that He controls everything, and He uses all circumstances for His glory and to advance His kingdom. He can even use sinful, horrible things to accomplish His purposes, exemplified by Jesus' crucifixion. How can you use God's sovereignty to help you overcome shame, regret, and anxiety? You don't have to control everything because God is in control. There is no Plan B for your life—God takes your failures and gloriously transforms them back into Plan A. Worship your Sovereign King.

3. When you marvel at the humility and meekness of Christ, your pride starts to melt away. How can you remind yourself of your infinite resources for humility and patient endurance when you are suffering (Colossians 1:11-14)? Picture yourself being welcomed into the love and glory of the Trinity. Picture "buckets" of grace being dumped on your head, and you will be able to love, serve, and forgive others. Let your heart be moved to thanksgiving for your inheritance, your redemption, and the forgiveness of your sins. Read these chapters and think more about humility: Psalms 3, 34, 40, 42, 43, 131, 133, Isaiah 53, Philippians 2, 1 Peter 2, Hebrews 2, 5, 13, and James 4.

4. How does Christ's decisive victory inspire you in your fight against sin? You are entering the battle with certain, ultimate victory. Is there any sin that Jesus cannot forgive and redeem? Relocate your identity into Christ and experience His victory every day. If you have a recurring sin that you are struggling with, get help from a trusted friend or counselor. We were never meant to fight alone (James 5:16).

5. How do you become more patient? It is good to ask God for patience every day. Admire patience in others. Think of Jesus' patience with you. Jesus is patiently waiting for His Bride right now. Christian maturity comes as we learn to discern good and evil (Hebrews 5:14), and as we allow the Holy Spirit to transform us through the Word of God. The Bible is your "plumb line" and you measure everything else by it (Isaiah 28:17).

6. Have you experienced church hurt? Have you ever seen church discipline done well? Pray for God to lead you in His wisdom. Sometimes we forgive and forget, sometimes we forgive and speak up, sometimes we forgive but leave the situation. Make sure you keep in mind that you are the worst sinner you know (1 Timothy 1:15), and experience God's grace for you before you go confront someone. Review Matthew 7:1-6 and talk about logs and specks. Everyone has something in their eye, and everyone needs help getting it out. Everyone started out with "piggish" thoughts of the gospel ("what's the use of a pearl, if it's not food?") until God showed you what a pearl it really is (Jesus' free gift of grace that changes everything).

7. How can you speak the truth in love? What is the difference between gossip and truthfully recounting a story about someone else? (Hint- it's judgment and passing a verdict.) When have you passed judgment on someone instead of coming alongside them? Are you stealing someone's reputation with your words? Our culture is not operating biblically: it accepts people declaring verdicts about others (name-calling), but does not accept declaring what is good and what is evil in someone's life (which is telling the truth in love). Let's be counter-cultural by speaking the truth in love without superiority, verdicts, or hit-and-run truth grenades.

8. Our words matter. Are you using your words to bless or to curse? Are you proclaiming God's excellence and glory to others? Ask God to give you words of life and encouragement, and repent of any words of jealousy, hatred, malice, gossip, or slander. Try to bless your family members and friends with your words every day. Call out the good that you see around you and praise God for all His mighty work in and through you.

The Church's One Foundation by Samuel John Stone

The Church's one foundation is Jesus Christ her Lord;
she is His new creation by water and the Word:
from heav'n He came and sought her to be His holy Bride;
with His own blood He bought her, and for her life He died.

Elect from every nation, yet one o'er all the earth,
her charter of salvation, one Lord, one faith one birth;
one holy Name she blesses, partakes one holy food,
and to one hope she presses, with every grace endued.

'Mid toil and tribulation, and tumult of her war,
she waits the consummation of peace forevermore;
till with the vision glorious, her longing eyes are blest,
and the great Church victorious shall be the Church at rest.

Yet she on earth hath union with God the Three in One,
and mystic sweet communion with those whose rest is won:
o happy ones and holy! Lord, give us grace that we,
like them the meek and lowly in love may dwell with Thee.

Chapter 10: Fight Sin with the Gospel: Envy, Discontentment, and Hatred are Toxic to Drink

Read Romans 6:12-14 and Titus 3:3.

Romans 6:12-14 "Let not sin therefore reign in your mortal body, to make you obey its passions. Do not present your members to sin as instruments for unrighteousness, but present yourselves to God as those who have been brought from death to life, and your members to God as instruments for righteousness. For sin will have no dominion over you, since you are not under law but under grace."

Titus 3:3 "For we ourselves were once foolish, disobedient, led astray, slaves to various passions and pleasures, passing our days in malice and envy, hated by others and hating one another."

1. Do you look down on other people for their sin? Is there one particular sin that you find so repulsive and heinous that you could never speak to someone who had done it? One offensive thing the Bible teaches is that we all are capable of every sin. It's the doctrine of Total Depravity, that we were all born with a broken, sin nature that is incapable of pleasing God. The doctrine of Common Grace means that God does not allow all people to be as sinful as they could be. Spend time praising God for His infinite love and grace that saves the worst sinners, making them children of God who can now please the Father. Repent of any superiority or inferiority you feel, and rise up in faith that you are forever clothed with Christ's righteousness and worthiness (Isaiah 61:10).

2. Contentment is a learned skill. It is delighting in God's work and plan for your life. It is sitting back and saying, "Christ Jesus has done all things well," including all the sorrow, hardship, joy and victory in your experience. How can you practice this skill every day? When something is bothering you, take it immediately to God in prayer. Remember that He approves of you, delights in you, and is with you now and forever. Painful things merit groaning, but repent quickly if you start grumbling against God because of your pain. Think of Jesus' pain that He suffered on your behalf and rejoice that you understand Jesus just a little bit better now.

3. Envy is all around us. Greed is almost impossible to see in yourself without someone else pointing it out to you. How can you fight against envy today? Try these three thoughts. First, God is providing everything you need that is good for you right now. Take a breath and let that sink in. Thank Him each time you use resources because He gave them to you. Second, ask God for correct desires. Remember how deceitful your heart is (Jeremiah 17:9). Try to go to the deep root of your desire: new jewelry may tell your heart that you feel worthy and significant, a new car could tell your heart that you are powerful, a big house may signify your proven worth to those who thought your were trash. You can find healing in Jesus who offers you worth, significance, beauty, power, and identity in Him apart from "stuff." Third, ask God to give you a generous heart instead. "For you know the grace of our Lord Jesus Christ, that though he was rich, yet for your sake he became poor, so that you by his poverty might become rich" (2 Corinthians 8:9). Think of all that you have in Jesus, and be generous with your time, money, and efforts. You will get a great return on investment in eternity.

4. What do you hate today? If you are growing in your faith, you will hate what God hates which is sin, injustice, and the enemy of God (Satan). We are told to love our enemies, so even though other people can sin against us and hurt us, we are not to hate another human. This is impossible without the work of the Holy Spirit in our hearts. Pray that you will love what God loves and hate what God hates today.

5. Are you drinking poison today? Envy, discontent, hatred, unforgiveness, resentment, and revenge are poison which will destroy you. Ask a friend if they see any of these things in you, and ask God to reveal them so you can repent. Drink from the river of delight instead. Read Psalm 36 and thank God for transforming you from being a wicked, deceitful person into a beloved child of God because of Jesus' willingness to die on the cross for you.

How Deep the Father's Love for Us by Stuart Townend

How deep the Father's Love for us, how vast beyond all measure,
that He should give His only Son to make a wretch His treasure.
How great the pain of searing loss, the Father turns His face away,
as wounds which mar the Chosen One bring many sons to glory.

Behold the Man upon the cross, my sin upon His shoulders,
ashamed, I hear my mocking voice call out among the scoffers.
It was my sin that held Him there until it was accomplished.
His dying breath has brought me life, I know that it is finished.

I will not boast in anything, no gifts, no power, no wisdom,
but I will boast in Jesus Christ, His death and resurrection.
Why should I gain from His reward? I cannot give an answer,
but this I know with all my heart:
His wounds have paid my ransom.

Chapter 11: Treasure Your Treasure: Delight in Jesus Every Day

Read Matthew 6:19-21 and Exodus 19:5-6.

Matthew 6:19-21 "Do not lay up for yourselves treasures on earth, where moth and rust destroy and where thieves break in and steal, but lay up for yourselves treasures in heaven, where neither moth nor rust destroys, and where thieves do not break in and steal. For where your treasure is, there your heart will be also."

Exodus 19:5-6 "Now therefore, if you will indeed obey my voice and keep my covenant, you shall be my treasured possession among all peoples, for all the earth is mine; and you shall be to me a kingdom of priests and a holy nation."

1. What do you treasure? What do you spend the majority of your time and money and efforts on? What benefit does your treasure offer you so that you love it so much? How can you see Jesus as your greatest treasure? What benefit do you receive from Jesus? Do you often think about heaven, or is your mind tied up in earthly things? Spend time reading Psalm 34 and worshiping God for the treasure you now have because of Jesus giving you the greatest gift of all: Himself.

2. What do you resonate with out of the examples of treasure: money, fame, beauty, or relationships? Ask God to show you anything that you have made into an idol in your heart. If you think you would die without that thing or person, then it could be an idol. You can daily remind yourself that God is more precious and powerful than anything else, and thank Him for His good plan for your life. Picture yourself holding everything in your life with open hands towards God. Job's words are so helpful: "Naked I came from my mother's womb, and naked I shall return. The LORD gave, and the LORD has taken away; blessed be the name of the LORD" (Job 1:21). God delights to bless you and establish you, and He will continue to bless you from now through eternity (Psalm 37:23-24).

3. How can your faith be more precious than all the gold in all the world (1 Peter 1:7-9)? The spiritual realm is so different from the physical realm. The invisible is more real than what you can see. Remind yourself of the infinite worth of God—therefore faith in Him is infinitely valuable, unlike anything in this world. Look at anything expensive and think, "My faith is infinitely more precious than that!"

4. What is the role of a priest? In the Old Testament, priests would bring the sacrifices of the people to God. They would intercede to God on behalf of the people. They would dedicate themselves to God's service and live a holy life. Do you think of yourself as a kingdom of priests to God? Praise God for giving you this new life mission of being an intercessor for others, a worshiper of God, and an ambassador of His message (2 Corinthians 5:20).

5. Would you like to live a frustration-free life? We live in a broken, sinful world, filled with inefficiency, mess-ups, and foolishness. Yet with just a little mental exercise, you can take a deep breath and move from discouraged, discontented and frustrated to delighted. Are you ready? All you have to do is adjust your expectations and assumptions. You are not entitled to a frustration-free existence. Your earthly life will never be as efficient and productive as you can imagine. Heaven is the place where you will see all your God-honoring dreams come true. Every time you encounter something that exasperates you, say to yourself, "This is not a surprise to God nor is it going to thwart His plan for me today. If my plans are failing today, God's plan is still moving forward. I will groan to God in this moment but I will not grumble (or curse) because He has given me ultimate victory in Christ. I will rejoice and delight in God's plan even if I am grieving my failed plan." You are forever welcomed to live in your safe place in Jesus' open arms.

Fairest Lord Jesus by Joseph Seiss

Fairest Lord Jesus! Ruler of all nature!
O Thou of God and man the Son!
Thee will I cherish, Thee will I honor,
Thou my soul's glory, joy, and crown!

Fair are the meadows, fairer still the woodlands,
robed in the blooming garb of spring:
Jesus is fairer, Jesus is purer, who makes the woeful heart to sing.

Fair is the sunshine, fairer still the moonlight,
and all the twinkling starry host:
Jesus shines brighter,
Jesus shines purer than all the angels heav'n can boast.

Beautiful Saviour! Lord of the nations!
Son of God and Son of Man!
Glory and honor, praise, adoration
now and forever more be Thine!

Chapter 12: Glory and Rest in Jesus: This is Where We Belong

Read Hebrews 4:9-16. Also read Psalm 95.

Hebrews 4:9-16 "So then, there remains a Sabbath rest for the people of God, for whoever has entered God's rest has also rested from his works as God did from his. Let us therefore strive to enter that rest, so that no one may fall by the same sort of disobedience. For the word of God is living and active, sharper than any two-edged sword, piercing to the division of soul and of spirit, of joints and of marrow, and discerning the thoughts and intentions of the heart. And no creature is hidden from his sight, but all are naked and exposed to the eyes of him to whom we must give account.

Since then we have a great high priest who has passed through the heavens, Jesus, the Son of God, let us hold fast our confession. For we do not have a high priest who is unable to sympathize with our weaknesses, but one who in every respect has been tempted as we are, yet without sin. Let us then with confidence draw near to the throne of grace, that we may receive mercy and find grace to help in time of need."

Psalm 95 "Oh come, let us sing to the LORD; let us make a joyful noise to the rock of our salvation! Let us come into his presence with thanksgiving; let us make a joyful noise to him with songs of praise! For the LORD is a great God, and a great King above all gods. In his hands are the depths of the earth; the hights of the mountains are his also. The sea is his, for he made it, and his hands formed the dry land. Oh come, let us worship and bow down; let us kneel before the LORD our Maker! For he is our God, and we are the people of his pasture, and the sheep of his hand. Today, if you hear his voice, do not harden your hearts, as at Meribah, as on the day at Massah in the wilderness, when your fathers put me to the test and put me to the proof, though they had seen my work. For forty years I loathed that generation and said, 'They are a people who go astray in their heart, and they have not known my ways.' Therefore I swore in my wrath, 'They shall not enter my rest.'"

1. Do you have a big God and small problems, or do you have big problems and a small "god"? Grumbling, forgetfulness, and complaining come more naturally to us than worshipping God. Try to think more about God and less about your problems. You belong to God, and He has promised to take care of you. Pray for eyes of faith to see this reality.

2. Do you see that God is enough? God rested on the seventh day, not because He was tired, but to admire His perfect work. He set that day aside and made it holy. When you take time to rest, you are declaring that God's work is perfect, and He is providing for you, not yourself. You can enjoy God's work and think about what He is doing in your life. You are no longer a slave! Let the Word of God expose your heart and motives, so that you can enjoy true rest now and ultimately when Jesus returns. Proclaim His greatness to others in community!

3. The Bible is all about glory. Have you thought about what glory means? The glory of God is the expression in our created world of His infinite excellence, His beauty, His worth and weightiness. We can reflect that glory to others, and we can give Him all the glory and praise of our lives. Can you see that everything in your life is all about glory? We are glory thieves, thinking that we can have glory for ourselves apart from God. Repent of stealing God's glory (sinning against others), of wanting man's glory, and of living for your own glory. Pray that God would receive the maximum glory in you and in those you love. Jesus lived for the glory of God: "Now is my soul troubled. And what shall I say? 'Father, save me from this hour'? But for this purpose I have come to this hour. Father, glorify your name" (John 12:27-28).

4. Where are you seeing the curse of fruitlessness in your life? The opposite of rest in Jesus is rebellion. Read Exodus 17:1-7 and Numbers 20:2-13. Do you relate to the grumbling and faithlessness of the children of Israel? God's holiness and power are so far above us—when the light of God exposes our rebellion, we can repent of our unbelief and worship Him. Jesus came to reverse the curse, making our work and our rest fruitful. Read John 15:1-17 and repent of any rebellion, and ask Jesus to help you abide in Him and bear fruit that lasts. Thank Jesus for being struck down so we can be grafted into the vine of the family of God.

5. Delight is wonderful! First, notice God so you can delight in Him. Next, picture Him noticing you and delighting in you because of Jesus. Realize that the delight of the Garden of Eden is now yours and even better: you have the righteousness and worthiness and rewards of Christ Himself for all eternity! Let Him wash away all your fears and anxieties, all your regrets and shame, all your uncertainty and doubt. God is writing you into His story. It will all be worth it in the end. "So we do not lose heart. Though our outer self is wasting away, our inner self is being renewed day by day. For this light momentary affliction is preparing for us an eternal weight of glory beyond all comparison, as we look not to the things that are seen, but to the things that are unseen. For the things that are seen are transient, but the things that are unseen are eternal" (2 Corinthians 4:16-18).

6. What are you listening to today? The Word of God is like a sharp sword or a surgeon's knife. It is the power of God in your life. You cannot live as a Christian without the Bible. When you hear His voice today, do not harden your heart but receive with meekness the Word of life. Your obedience to God brings pleasure to Him. Let Him expose the cancerous growths of pride and self-righteousness in your life, and rejoice in the new humility, meekness, patience, and wisdom that He creates. Make sure you are in the Word every day. Memorize verses so you can take them with you everywhere you go. Read the Word out loud whenever you can. The way to your heart is through your ears (Hebrews 3:15-4:2), so be careful how you listen.

The Love of God by F.M. Lehman

The love of God is greater far than tongue or pen can ever tell.
It goes beyond the highest star and reaches to the lowest hell.
The guilty pair, bowed down with care, God gave His Son to win;
His erring child He reconciled, and pardoned from his sin.

When hoary time shall pass away,
and earthly thrones and kingdoms fall;
when men who here refuse to pray,
on rocks and hills and mountains call;
God's love so sure, shall still endure, all measureless and strong;
redeeming grace to Adam's race- the saints' and angels' song.

Could we with ink the ocean fill,
and were the skies of parchment made;
were ev'ry stalk on earth a quill, and every man a scribe by trade;
to write the love of God above would drain the ocean dry;
nor could the scroll contain the whole
though stretched from sky to sky.

O love of God, how rich and pure! How measureless and strong!
It shall forevermore endure- the saints' and angels' song.

Chapter 13: Epilogue

You can use the epilogue in the book as a daily prayer just by rephrasing the sentences and talking to God about each thought. Please pray for me too as you pray for yourself and others. I am so glad we are family in Jesus, and for eternity we will tell each other all the stories of God's faithfulness and redemption.

Thanks so much for reading this study guide! I love hearing your feedback, and I would love to serve you with more biblical resources. You can visit me and connect at janetabadir.com.

A Debtor to Mercy Alone by Augustus Toplady

A debtor to mercy alone, of covenant mercy I sing,
nor fear, with God's righteousness on,
my person and off'rings to bring.
The terrors of law and of God
with me can have nothing to do;
my Savior's obedience and blood
hide all my transgressions from view.

The work which His goodness began,
the arm of His strength will complete;
His promise is Yea and Amen,
and never was forfeited yet.
Things future, nor things that are now,
not all things below or above,
can make Him his purpose forgo, or sever my soul from His love.

My name from the palms of His hands, eternity will not erase;
imprest on His heart, it remains
in marks of indelible grace.
Yes! I to the end shall endure, as sure as the earnest is giv'n;
more happy, but not more secure,
the souls of the blessed in heav'n.

About the Author

Janet S. Abadir MD practiced general surgery for 24 years before becoming a writer, Bible teacher, speaker, and coach. She and her husband and three teenage sons live in Kodiak, Alaska, and attend Frontier Baptist Church.

She has been called to speak the message of freedom to God's people. Her extensive knowledge of scripture, paired with professional skills and compassionate love for others, equip her as a powerful instrument for God's kingdom in her community.

For more information, contact her at JanetAbadir.com

DRINK FROM THE RIVER OF DELIGHT

WELCOME TO GOD'S HEALING SPACE IN HIS WORD

What is Keeping You From Delight?

Feeling empty? Need to reconnect with your sense of vitality and purpose? Believing in Jesus can change your day-to-day life into the **extraordinary, significant, and glorious** adventure you desire.

Find the resources you need right now in God and His Word. Freedom and healing begin today.

Drink from the River of Delight shows your biblical concepts that will transform your faith from dreary and lackluster to **vibrant, passionate, and empowered**.

The Bible is God's word, and has the power you have been searching for to change your life. In *Drink from the River of Delight*, Dr. Abadir uses the Bible like a surgeon's knife to expose and heal the deepest places of your heart. Your life will be transformed as you see the beauty of the gospel of Jesus Christ, and hear the voice of God speaking into your situation, **bringing healing, joy, and delight**.

You will also see how safe you are in God. You are welcomed and wanted in **God's safe, healing space**, which you will find in His word.

Inside, you will find the way to a life of delight and freedom in God:
-Dr. Abadir's inspiring story of God's transforming power in her life
-Bible passages that will speak to the deepest longings of your heart
-Tools to fight perfectionism, and foundational principles for understanding the Bible
-Essential concepts you need to thrive in your church
-Worship prompts, ideas for prayer and journaling

www.ingramcontent.com/pod-product-compliance
Lightning Source LLC
Chambersburg PA
CBHW021146060526
44107CB00146B/1327/J